Not Worms!

by Margaret Watts

illustrated by Greg Gaul

Harcourt Achieve

Rigby • Saxon • Steck-Vaughn

www.HarcourtAchieve.com   1.800.531.5015

Characters

 Steffy

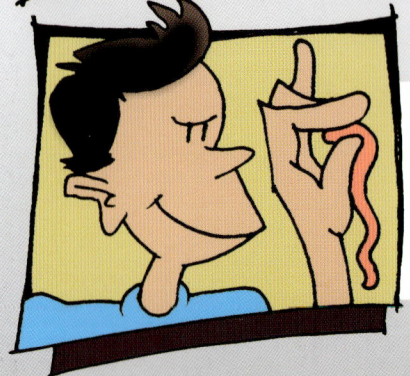 Colin

 Mom

Contents

Chapter 1
Grumbles   4

Chapter 2
It's Cold Outside   10

Chapter 3
No Help!   14

Chapter 4
A Saucy Trick   22

Chapter 1

Grumbles

"Wash your hands," said Colin.

"Why?" asked Steffy.

"Because Mom said dinner is ready," Colin told her. "Don't you want any?"

Steffy pulled a face. "We had cabbage yesterday. Yuck! Today we're having broccoli. Double yuck!"

"Vegetables are good for you," Colin said.

"Good for worms and caterpillars," grumbled Steffy.

Steffy looked up and saw a bird gliding across the sky. "I wish I could be a bird." She spread her arms wide like wings.

Colin laughed. "What kind?"

"A bird with a big bill and wide wings. I'd fly so high our house would look tiny, like a little painted block. And *you* would be as teeny as an ant."

"You'd have to watch out for planes up there," Colin teased.

"I know that," Steffy said as she zoomed around the yard on her tiptoes. She flapped her arms like wings.

"I'd fly all day. When I was tired, I'd come down and float on the river. I'd never, *never* eat anything I didn't like."

"You wouldn't like being a bird," said Colin.

"I would so," said Steffy. "It would be cool. I would never have to brush my teeth or wash my hands."

Chapter 2

It's Cold Outside

"You'd be cold at night," Colin warned.

"No, I wouldn't." Steffy stroked her arms. "I'd have heaps of feathers. They would keep me toasty warm."

"Well, what about TV? You wouldn't be able to watch it," Colin said.

"Yes, I would. I could sit on the window sill and peek in," Steffy chirped.

"Not with the curtains closed, silly."

Steffy stuck her nose in the air.
"I wouldn't want to watch TV," she said. "I'd be too busy having fun."

"I would go to the South Pole and play leapfrog with the penguins. Then I'd fly to an amusement park, go on all the rides, and play catch with friends," said Steffy.

"Not if you were a bird." Colin roared with laughter. "Birds can't catch. They don't have hands."

"Will you please hurry up?" their mother called. "I want you two to set the table."

"All right, Mom," said Colin as they went inside. Steffy flapped her arms as she followed him.

No Help!

Colin began to put out the knives and forks. All Steffy did was swoop around the room.

"Come and put out the plates," Colin said.

Steffy shook her head. "You said that birds don't have hands. So how can I carry plates?"

"Stop it," Colin yelled. "Come and help me."

Steffy perched on the arm of a chair. She tucked her hands in her armpits to make a pair of wings. "Birds don't need tables and chairs. They just eat on the ground or on a branch."

"You would hate bird food," Colin told her.

Steffy put her head to one side like a robin. "I think I would like it," she said. "And since I'd be a bird, nobody could tell me what to eat."

Steffy stuck out her neck. "I could go to a mango tree or a banana farm. I could eat and eat until I was stuffed full." She laughed loudly like a kookaburra.

Colin was fed up. "Cut it out," he yelled.

"I'm a little, yellow canary sitting high up in a tree. I can sing all day because I can do whatever I please," Steffy sang.

Steffy tried to sing like a canary. It sounded more like a fork scraping the bottom of a pot. Colin put his hands over his ears.

"Stop making that noise!" Colin ordered.

"All right," said Steffy. She hopped down from the chair. Her skinny legs took long, careful steps. She ducked her head as she walked like a flamingo.

Steffy was having a good time. She didn't even notice when Colin dashed out of the room. She only looked up when her mother came in.

"Dinner is ready," Mom said as she put a big bowl of spaghetti on the table.

Chapter 4

A Saucy Trick

"Spaghetti! Wow!" Steffy forgot all about being a bird.

"That smells so yummy — I could eat the whole bowl," Steffy said as she rushed to her chair.

Colin walked back into the room.

"Oh, no, you don't!" he said as he took away Steffy's bowl. In its place he put a plastic plate. On it were two long, thin shapes. They were a dark red color.

Steffy stared. "What's that?"

"Your dinner," said Colin.

Steffy gave Colin a puzzled look. "What are they?"

"Two tasty worms," said Colin.

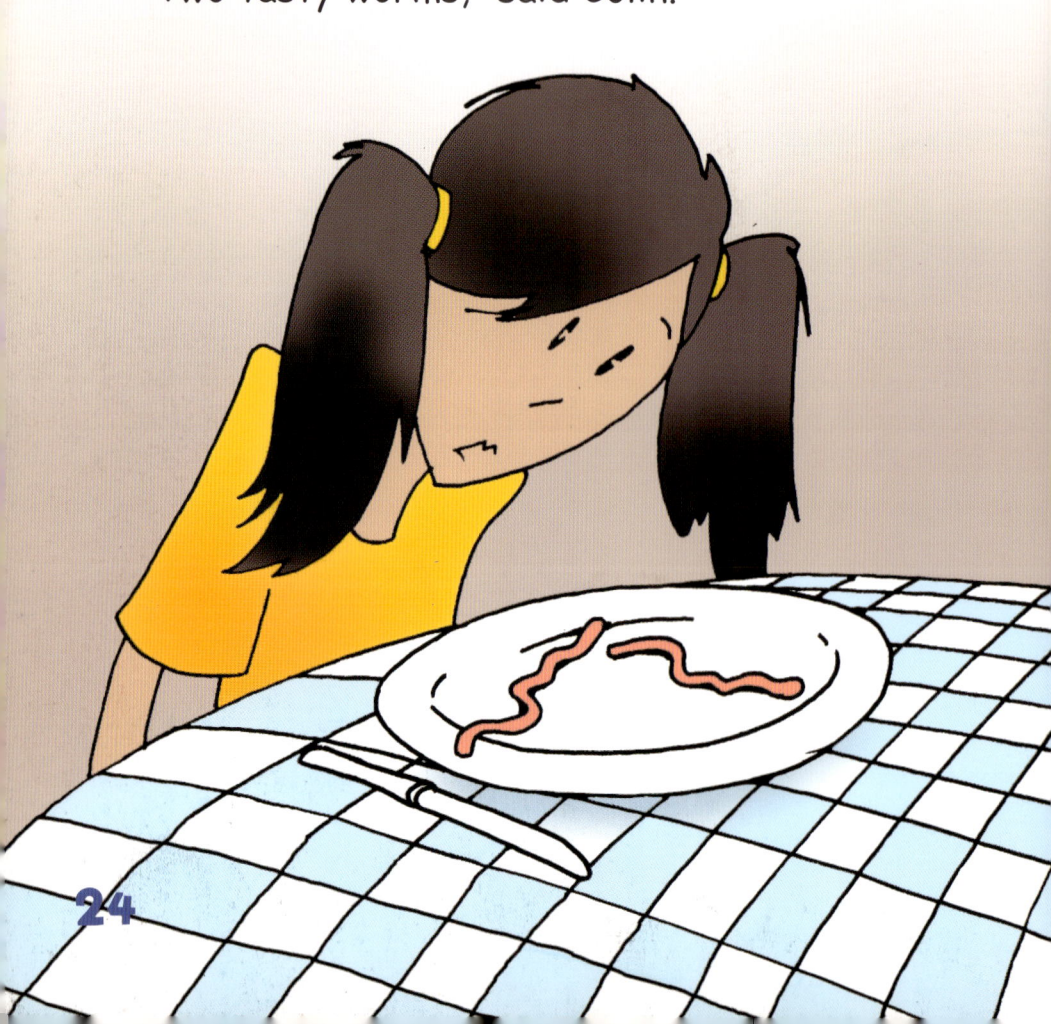

With a squeal, Steffy sprang to her feet. "Take them away," she shouted. "Take them away!"

"You said you liked bird food," Colin reminded her.

"I didn't mean worms," Steffy shrieked.

"Why don't you try them?" asked Colin. "You might like them."

"You eat them!" she said and shoved the plate across the table.

"All right, I will." Colin picked up a worm in each hand. He opened his mouth and swallowed one and then the other. Steffy stared bug-eyed.

Colin patted his stomach. "Yum! That was tasty," he said. "I wish I had some more."

"Yuck," cried Steffy, putting a hand over her mouth. Her face was turning green. She rushed off to the bathroom.

Just then, their mother came back into the room. "Who used the tomato sauce?" she asked.

"Me," grinned Colin. "I used the sauce to cover some spaghetti. I made some yummy, fat *spaghetti* worms."

Glossary

bug-eyed
when eyes are large with surprise

chirped
made a short, high-pitched sound like a bird

gliding
floating on air currents

perched
resting on the edge of something

stroked
moved hands gently over an object

swoop
to move down quickly like a bird

teeny
tiny

zoomed
flew very quickly

Margaret Watts

My favorite spaghetti joke:

"Waiter, waiter!" shouted a customer.

The waiter hurried over.

"Yes, Sir?" he said.

"How long will my spaghetti be?"

"I'll see," said the waiter, and off he went to the kitchen.

At last the waiter returned.

"Well, how long will it be?" demanded the angry customer.

"About eight inches," said the waiter.

Greg Gaul

ILLUSTRATOR ATTEMPTS TO FLY